The Holmes Family in Akron

Norma J. Wright

Copyright © 2024 by Norma J Wright

All rights reserved. No part of this publication may be reproduced, stored or transmitted in any form or by any means, electronic, mechanical, photocopying, recording, scanning, or otherwise without written permission from the publisher. It is illegal to copy this book, post it to a website, or distribute it by any other means without permission.

Some image(s) used are produced by ProQuest LLC as part of ProQuest® Historical Newspapers.www.proquest.com.

Norma J Wright has no responsibility for the persistence or accuracy of URLs for external or third-party Internet Websites referred to in this publication and does not guarantee that any content on such Websites is, or will remain, accurate or appropriate.

First edition

Dedicated to my Dad who had the patience to tell the stories again and again

Contents

I   Foreword

1   Introduction
2   The Early Years (1870-1903)
3   They Moved Many Times (1903-1930)
    Addison
4   33 Chase Court (1930-1950)
    Norman
    Mary Exalted Temple No. 95 and The Optimistic 50, 1943
5   Tying Up The Loose Ends
    Fannie Hughes Cleveland and the NAAMHC
    The Cincinnati Connection
    The Detroiters and John E W Thompson
6   Afterword
    Our August vacations
    Where did it all go?
7   Photographs
8   Bibliography

II   Addendum

9   Tracing A Family History Using Newspaper Accounts
    Introduction
    An Intriguing Beginning
    Discoveries
    Analyzing These Discoveries

I

Foreword

The family name in the title of this paper is a misnomer but trying to name this family is difficult because it mostly follows the women in the family. They would all marry and so their family name would change. In any case, this is a chronological account (mostly) of the family starting with Julia Louisa Hughes from the time she escaped from slavery until her granddaughter Ethel moved to Cleveland in the early 1950s.

1

Introduction

I drove to Akron for an evening in May of 2012. I planned on leaving the next day, after spending a few hours at their public library, to pick up my son from the University of Pittsburgh. As a settled in that evening in a local hotel, I turned to the local PBS station. They had a documentary of Akron on. I was surprised as it reached its end to see the only person of color mentioned was Sojourner Truth. The honorary mention was about the speech she gave in Akron. No other person of color is mentioned in the whole piece. [Sidebar: Sojourner is buried in Battle Creek, where my family was stationed in the 1950s.] My main purpose in writing this story and documenting the Holmes family in Akron is to make sure Akron has more than Sojourner's speech or the McClain manuscript to document the lives of those who lived and prospered in spite of the many challenges they faced. I'm almost sure members of my family are there listening to Miss Truth. Most of the early members of Akron aren't doctors and lawyers; they are porters, drayman, laborers, cooks, and domestics.

The best of these worked for the Seiberlings, Perkins and Firestones. They built the Akron upon which drew new peoples of color and other skilled and unskilled labor that came flocking to the Rubber City. Documenting the lives of the Holmes family is the focus of this book and is in turn, a look into the lives of ordinary people.

It would be helpful to introduce the main family members this book covers, briefly First, Sarah (Sadie) Glover (nee Hughes) and her husband William Glover. Her children are Raymond, Ethel, Addison (Manny) and Sadie Mae. Sarah's cousin Fanny Cleveland (nee Hughes) and her husband, George Cleveland also spent time in Akron. The offspring of Ethel, William and Norman (my father) are also mentioned in the book. Other families of note, including those who are in-laws of one sort or other, are the Parrishes, Davises, Greens, Hailstocks and Scruggs.

The main sources used are the Akron Beacon Journal (ABJ) and the city directories from the Akron Summit Public Library (going back to the 1870s when my people arrived). They are a great source of the Hughes family's movements and the jobs they held. Another major resource is the Cleveland Call and Post. There are also primary sources such as w2s, letters of recommendation from places of work, pictures and other pieces of their lives such as insurance papers, etc. A great debt is also owed to my cousin Marc, whose mother Sadie was the keeper of all things. Having seen the wealth of his collection that he as either shared or given to me is immeasurable.

The influence of who the family worked for may have had some influence on their societal level and influence. My grandmother, Ethel, worked for families of the Firestone Company and her mother, the Seiberlings (founders of Goodyear). Addison, Ethel's brother, worked at the Akron Hotel. My father, Norman, worked at Goodyear and at the Mathews Hotel. Ethel's other brother Raymond was a mechanic and chauffer like his father William who worked as a drayman or coachman which may be the more familiar term. These connections, particularly to the Seiberlings I believe, made the family's life easier. Not easy, but easier. When Addison was 'in trouble' by accounts published in the Akron Beacon Journal, his punishments seemed to be lessened. We (Marc and I) believe this was on account of Sarah Glover's (Ethel's mother) relationship with them. There is no documentation of how deep it was, but Ethel was married in the Seiberling building and I'm sure with approval of the owners.

INTRODUCTION

The Akron Beacon Journal (or ABJ as it is familiarly

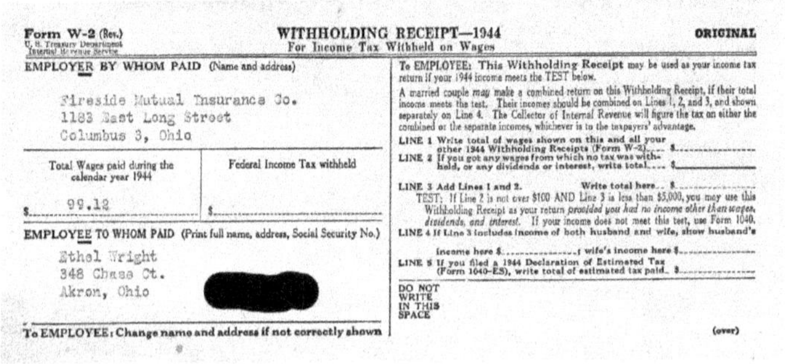

Figure 1: W-2 form for wages earned by Ethel Wright in 1944. Provided by author.

referred to) was the first Akron newspaper to document people of color and is the only one still around with archives before 1930. There were local black newspapers. Alexander Davis, a cousin-in-law ran a printing shop and a newspaper for a time, but most were small and limited in years. For a time, the ABJ had a colored reporter Hannibal B Lyons and a special section which reported news of importance. When he was not reporting the news, there seemed to be biases (and I use that term generously) that were printed in full force.

For example, there were two pictures of Norman in the Akron Beacon Journal during the Soap Box Derby in the 1930s. My grandmother kept only the first one. The second was so racially bigoted, it was totally

INTRODUCTION

understandable that she didn't keep it.

Other members of my family were mentioned from the early 1870s through the 1950s. Some of these articles involved the organizations Ethel and Sadie were members of. Early events covered some of the activism of George Cleveland, a first cousin-in-law to Sarah. Some were just social notes of the comings and goings, birthday parties and neighborhood events. Either way, my family seemed to have more than their fair share of publicity. Marc and I surmised much of this publicity was because of the family's early arrival and their foothold near white society (even if it was from the back door of their house). Of course, there were parades at which the Black Elks otherwise known as in Improved Benevolent and Protective Order of the Elks) and their band participated regularly that were not covered, and where local sororities and fraternities had regular social events. I will say, the Elks Lodge was home to many events based on the pictures, I have. But this (like the many other social avenues) is not the focus of this story. Akron was booming and so were the colored people. Somehow, over time, that was all filtered out of the ABJ. In the 1930s through 50s, thanks to the Cleveland Call and Post, an African American newspaper, Akronites could post their events as they were happening in their neighborhoods. It is a large part of documenting their story. Even my father

INTRODUCTION

probably didn't know about all of the postings of him.

Where to start? Well, the beginning, with the arrival of Julia and Addison Holmes.

Julia Louisa Hughes was an escaped slave originally from Virginia. She was born around 1835 to Julia and Levin Hughes. She was sold off along with perhaps two other daughters of this union around 1845. Stories passed down say she escaped North from Kentucky sometime before 1850 where she settled in Cincinnati. She had a relationship with Moses Johnston which produced two known children, Louisa and William. She left Cincinnati most likely because of the Fugitive Slave Law and spent some time in Canada. However, at the time of this writing no documentation can be found as to where in Canada she lived. Upon the news of the Emancipation Proclamation, it is believed she returned with Addison Holmes to Toledo where documentation can be found of her living there in 1864 (City Directories for Toledo, OH). This is also where Sarah Holmes, their daughter, was born in 1863. Addison would join the USCT (United States Colored Troops) in 1864 as a substitute and serve attached to the Army of the Tennessee for the remainder of the Civil War. They would arrive in Akron in the 1870s.

2

The Early Years (1870-1903)

The first city directory record of the Holmes family in Akron is 1871-2 ("Historic City Directories | Special Collections"), residing at High and Main. They would be one of the first colored families documented in Akron—which included the Hailstocks and the Greens—as there were no more than 200 listed in the 1870 directory (Kingsberry, Akron Negro Directory). From 1871-1881 Addison worked as a cook moving his family to several places. He was most likely working at the Empire Hotel which the 1873-4 directory shows.

> AKRON DIRECTORY. 59
>
> Hollower Jacob, carpenter S Perkins.
> Holmes Addison, cook, res w s High e Main.
> Holmes Mrs Huldah, res 106 N Broadway.
> Holmes James, pattern maker, res 106 N Broadway
> Holstein Nathan L, cigar maker 192 S Main, res 104 E Middlebury.

Figure 2: Bailey's Akron Directory 1871-72.

They moved several times, first to the southwest corner of High and Main Street, then to the southside of Ridge and High, then to 230 East Furnace St and

> **Chipman & Barnes** Manufacture every.
>
> 76   AKRON DIRECTORY.
>
> Holloway J K, physician and surgeon, office 125 E Exchange, res w s Main n Thornton
> Holloway John W, master mechanic, C Mt V & C R R, res 109 S Prospect
> Holmes Addison, laborer, res e s Robinson n High. 6th ward.
> Holmes Addison, cook, Empire House, res s s Ridge w High.
> Holmes James, pattern maker, res e s Broadway n Market

Figure 3: A.R. Talcott&Sons City Directory, 1874, pg. 76.

finally to 118 Cuyahoga St. During this ten-year period, (Julia) Louisa, his wife, would find her mother, Julia Hughes alive in Virginia. She would bring her to Akron to live with her (Wright, Norma).

On Dec 7, 1881, the Summit Beacon reported Addison had died of heart disease ("Death Notice: Addison Holmes").

"Mr. Addison Holmes, colored, 118 Cuyahoga Street died very suddenly Friday morning of heart disease." -7 Dec 1881, Summit Beacon Journal

However, the recording of his death in the probate office of Summit County reported he died of tuberculosis, though he could have died from both. He was just 59 years old.

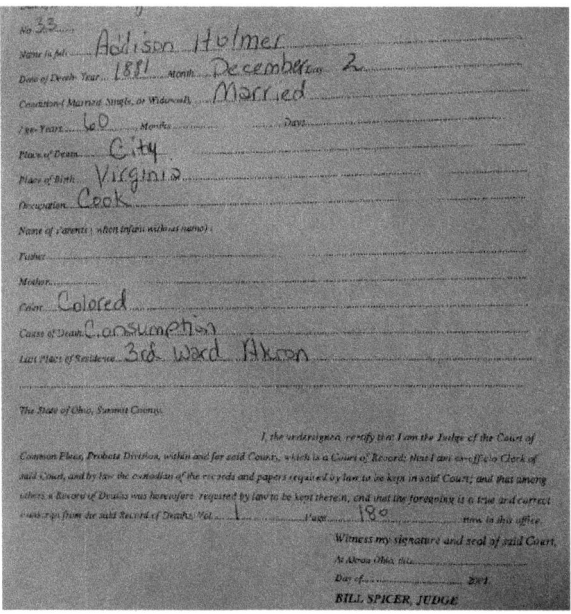

Figure 4: Uncertified copy of Death Record obtained from Probate Office, Akron Ohio. Vol. 1 page 180.

(Julia) Louisa continued to live on Cuyahoga Street with her daughter, Sarah. The 1884 directory shows Louisa worked at H&A Kepler's Laundry most likely as a washerwoman. Between 1885-1887, she and Sadie (Sarah's nickname),

THE EARLY YEARS (1870-1903)

moved from 114 Cuyahoga to 116 Cuyahoga Street. In 1886, Sarah married William Glover, listed as a cook in the 1887 directory. They had a son, Raymond, who was born in Rockville, Indiana on 19th June 1886 according to his death certificate. Whether the family was on the road at that time is not certain. In May of 1886 Sarah met her older sister, Louisa Johnson Cleveland ("Sarah Meets Sister"), who lived in Cincinnati for the first time. During these years, there were

> "Mrs. William Glover, of the North End, has returned from a happy visit to friends in Cincinnati where she had the peculiar pleasure of being greeted by a married sister whom she had never heretofore seen."

a few reunions with family that had been separated because of the institution of slavery and the Fugitive Slave Act of 1850. Sarah and Louisa would maintain their relationship over the years which would be advantageous to Sarah's daughters.

> "Mrs. Sadie Glover, of 180 North Broadway, was surprised Monday night by a few of her friends who called in honor of her 26th birthday. She received some very handsome presents, and after a most bounteous repast the guest left at a late hour, after having spent a delightful time." - *Summit County Beacon, 26 May 1889*

It must have been quite the birthday bash to have been

reported to the papers. She had just had her second child, Ethel, who was born on 20 Feb 1889. Less than a year later, on the 28th of Nov 1890, the Akron Beacon Journal reported the death of William Glover, Sarah's husband, at the age of 30.

> "William Glover, who died insane at the infirmary, leaves a widow, also a son and daughter, the former five and the latter two years of age. The family are living with Mrs. Holmes, mother of the widow, at the North End. Upon Mrs. Glover rest the burden, as it has for several months, of earning support for herself and little ones. Glover had been in the service as coachman of a number of Akron's wealthiest families, and was esteemed a very reliable man." *Akron Beacon Journal, 28 Nov 1890*

His reported cause of death, insanity, was a well-kept secret from younger members of the family. There could have been many causes for his illness. From the account, though he had been sick for a few months, the onset seemed sudden. She would never marry again, though her later children were from well-formed relationships both before and after William. Raymond would later tell his nephew, Marcus, "they were all Glovers" though their fathers were not all the same.

THE EARLY YEARS (1870-1903)

By 1891, (Sarah)Sadie Glover and (Julia)Louisa Holmes had moved to 152 North Summit Street. She and (Julia) Louisa again moved in 1892, to 148 North Summit. On 21st Sep 1893, Louisa married Christopher Bailey, who worked for the Taplin Rice & Company. Christopher was a recent 'widower' and was also in demand as a single, widowed male.

[From my research, being reportedly widowed doesn't mean, divorced. It seems, at least in this family, they had a habit of leaving (divorcing) without getting papers and then remarrying. Divorces would be reported in the newspaper, but I found no such records of divorce or death of their partner for Christopher Bailey or Ethel Glover. In fact, Christopher had to appear in court in February of 1889 for attempting to obtain a marriage license before a divorce. Christopher professed to not wanting to marry another person ("A License to Wed Before the Divorce Is Granted").]

"A LICENSE TO WED BEFORE THE DIVORCE WAS GRANTED.
From Saturday's Daily Beacon
Sometime ago Mrs. Amanda Molton brought suit in Common Pleas Court for a divorce from her husband John Molton. The couple are well known colored people of Akron. The divorce case was heard yesterday

about noon, but the divorce was not granted. During the afternoon yesterday, Christopher Bailey, colored made his appearance in Probate Court and procured a marriage license for himself and a Amanda Peterson, the same woman above mentioned. This morning Bailey reappeard in Probate Courte and asked Judge Grant to take the license back as he had learned that the divorce was not granted. Judge Grant said to Bailey that he had already sworn that the woman had no other husband living and that was sufficient to send him to the penitentiary once and if he married her he could be sent up again. Bailey's knees knocked together and his eyes protruded as he said "Good Lord, Boss, take de paper back, I don want it. You can keep de money, but take the paper back." The Judge told he had better keep it, that if Amanda get her divorce he might marry her. Bailey said he had been married three times already and he didn't dare to be married any more anyhow". *-February 13, 1889, Summit Beacon Journal*

Christopher Bailey was a Civil War veteran, originally living in Cuyahoga Falls and had children from his previous marriage. Once married to Louisa, the family moved to 141 1/2 Grant Street in 1893, then 197 North High and in 1895 to 117 E Furnace

THE EARLY YEARS (1870-1903)

Street.

During this time Julia Hughes, Louisa's mother, left Akron to return to Virginia sometime between late 1886 and 1890. If an account in the paper is true, in September of 1886, another daughter of Julia's came to Akron to visit. It was her intention to bring her home to Virginia. Julia had grown homesick after staying in Akron and wanted to return to Virginia. Julia Hughes would eventually return to Akron around 1899 where she shows up again in the 1900 Akron City Directory. She would stay in Akron with her daughter, (Julia) Louisa, until her death in 1902.

> "Mrs B. Taylor, of Alexandria, Va., is visiting her mother Mrs. Julia Hughes and sister Mrs. Louisa Holmes, of 116 Cuyahoga street, whom she has not seen for 12 years. She expects to take her mother home with her."-*Akron Beacon Journal, 8 Sep 1886*

To date, we haven't been able to identify Mrs. Taylor. She and another daughter, Mrs. Julia Elyard would come to Akron to reunite with their mother and sister.

> "Mrs. Sadie Glover, after visiting in Alexandria, Va., and Washington, D.C., for two weeks has returned home bringing with her Mrs. Julia Hughes, her grandmother."-Akron Beacon Journal, ca.1899

One of the few undated clippings from the newspapers, but this is when Julia returned to Akron to stay. One can also assume, Sadie met her Virginia relatives during this trip.

In 1897, the family moved to 190 1/2 N Broadway where they settled down. Christopher Bailey would pass in 1899. With the marriage of Christopher and Louisa, the family was afforded some stability and after his death the women would still be able to maintain their residence.

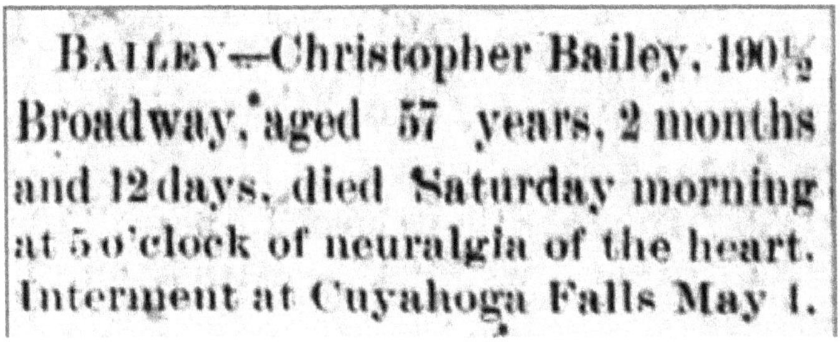

> BAILEY—Christopher Bailey, 190½ Broadway, aged 57 years, 2 months and 12 days, died Saturday morning at 5 o'clock of neuralgia of the heart. Interment at Cuyahoga Falls May 1.

Figure 5: Death notice for Christopher Bailey, Louisa Hughes' last husband -Akron Daily Democrat 29 Apr 1899

> "Ill but Twenty Hours – The funeral of Christopher Bailey, aged 57 years, who died Saturday of neuralgia of the heart, at his home, 190 ½ North Broadway, was jeld Monday afternoon at 2 o'clock from A.M.E. Zion church. Mr. Bailey's illness was of but 20 hours' duration. He had been in the employ of Taplin, Rice & Company for 30 years." –

THE EARLY YEARS (1870-1903)

Akron Beacon Journal 15 Apr 1899

At 190 1/2 N Broadway, Sarah Glover would become life-long friends with Aura Davis of Mobile, Alabama who lived in the other half of 190 North Broadway. The arranged marriages by these two women and their counterparts from the families of the Greens, Parrish's, Davis', Christians, Hailstocks and the Glovers would build a community of black Akronites that last until this day.

(Sarah) Sadie, her four children, Julia Hughes (her grandmother), and her mother, (Julia) Louisa, would stay at this address until 1903. Julia Hughes would pass in February 1902. The Akron Democrat would have a front-page article about her. A shorter version of Julia Hughes's death was published in the Akron Beacon Journal on 4th March 1902. Sarah's mother, (Julia) Louisa Bailey, would pass on July 4th, 1902.

THE EARLY YEARS (1870-1903)

George and Fannie Hughes Churchwell

In 1899, Sarah's cousin, Fannie Hughes Churchwell and her husband, George Churchwell, came to reside in Akron at 153 Maiden Lane. George worked as a teamster. Fannie had traveled to Akron to visit her Aunt Julia in the 1880s. She was captured along with Julia on the 1880 census in Akron. She was about the same age as Sarah, having been born in 1861. She married George Churchwell in Washington, DC in 1887. They had a daughter, Elna, who was called Naomi in 1894. Ethel, Sarah's oldest daughter and Naomi would become close cousins. Once in Akron, George Churchwell became involved in the social and cultural clubs of the day. Of these was the Loyal Legion of Labor (LLL) and the Akron Progressive Club, where he served as President. Fannie would also be involved as a Heart of the LLL.

THE EARLY YEARS (1870-1903)

A Bazar Given Tuesday by Loyal Legion

"A bazar for charity was given Tuesday evening by the members of the Loyal Legion of Labor. It was given in True Reformers' hall on South Howard street, and was attended. About $20, the proceeds of the bazar, was turned over to Poor Director Kendall. An interesting program as given in connection with the bazar. Solos were sung by Misses Sarah Thomas and Lillian Rogers and addresses were given by Dr. F. H. Simpson,Z. W Mitchell and **George Churchwell**."

Figure 6: The LLL was founded in Springfield, Ohio and had a column in the ABJ. 21 Jan 1903, Akron Beacon Journal.

Progressive Club
Akron Colored Men Organized It Monday

The Akron Progessive club was organized at 307 North Howard street Monday night.

The club is a negro organization and has about 60 members. The object of the club is to assist in the upbuilding and education of the negro race. The organization will meet every Monday night. An effort will be made to make the club prominent socially. An entertainment is contemplated in the near future. The club elected the following officers: President, **George Churchwell**; vice president, William Bowles; secretary, William Archer; assistant secretary, William Walker; treasurer, Elijah Christian; advocate, James Alexander; sergeant at arms, Floyd Newberry; corresponding secretary, Robert Howard.

Figure 7: Start of the Progressive Club, 21 Oct 1907, Akron

THE EARLY YEARS (1870-1903)

Beacon Journal

George Churchwell, Fannie's husband takes the helm of the of the newly formed Akron Progressive Club. Another prominent name in the Holmes' extended 'family' is Elijah Christian whose family members would marry into the Green family."Members of the Loyal Legion of Labor held a charity bazar at True Reformers' hall, S. Howard st. Solos were sung by the Misses Sarah Thomas and Lillian Robers. Addresses were delivered by Z. W. Mitchell, George Churchwell and Dr. F.H. Simpson. Proceeds were turned over to Poor Director Kendall."

Figure 8: 24 Jan 1908 Akron Beacon Journal

After 1928, George 'disappears' from the written record of the Loyal Legion and other organizations. Though no record of death can be located, it is assumed he passed away sometime thereafter. Although Ohio death records have been fairly well-kept, there is no definitive record of his death. The only record found lists the name of a 'George Churchill' who dies in a Cleveland jail in 1932 with no real identifying information to suggest he is George Churchwell other than matching the age of 62.

Eventually, Fannie Churchwell follows her daughter to Detroit sometime before 1930. Cousins Fannie and Naomi would continue to be known throughout the generations. They would continue to visit Akron over the years. Cousin Fannie would die in Detroit in 1950 at the age of 88. Naomi is seen living with her cousin, Ethel, on 1920 census. Naomi would marry Andrew

THE EARLY YEARS (1870-1903)

Young in 1919 but have no children. Naomi would pass away in 1972 at the age of 72.

3

They Moved Many Times (1903-1930)

In 1903, Sarah and her family moved to 118 North Broadway. Her eldest daughter, Ethel, would leave for Wilberforce College in September 1904, but then marry William Royal (Ransom) Green in February, 1905. They would have a child, James Theo who was born early on 30 May 1905, but would die on November 13, 1905. They would all move to 186 E Mill Street. Raymond Glover, Ethel's brother would work as a janitor; William as a porter. Their second son, Oliver William Raymond would be born in Dec 1906. William and Ethel would leave shortly after for Youngstown, Ohio. Ethel would not return to live in Akron until after the death of her second husband, Henry Wright in 1925.

Figure 9: William and Ethel Green with their son, James Theo ca. 1905.

THEY MOVED MANY TIMES (1903-1930)

THE HOLMES FAMILY IN AKRON

Raymond would become the head of the family working as a porter at Isemann & Corbin. In 1908, Raymond would move the family to 189 Hill St. He too, would eventually leave Akron following his sister, Ethel, to Youngstown where they both can be found on the 1910 census. He would return to Akron in 1913 with Mattie (Martha) Clark, his new wife. They would move in with the rest of the family. He became employed at the HobNob Club. In 1918, Ray and Mattie would move to Fuller Street and he would start his career at Cleveland Cadillac Company eventually becoming a chauffeur. Meanwhile, Sarah Glover moved to 113 Lincoln Street in 1917 with Addison Emmanuel and Sadie Mae. Addison would be called to serve in WWI, but was honorably discharged because of a medical condition and he returned to Akron. Sarah was employed as a janitress at the Union Depot. The family continued to have social news publicized mostly in the ABJ. On Jan 2, 1914, the Akron Beacon Journal reported on the Hailstocks (another family in which the (Aura) Davis' would marry into) New Year's Eve party which Sarah attended. There was also a report on Sarah's return to health following a bout of rheumatism.

"Mrs. Sadie Glover of Hill street, who has been a victim of rheumatism all Winter is reported much better."

Figure 10: The last entry in the local News column of Akron's Negro Citizens 10 Feb 1914, Akron Beacon Journal

"Miss Ethel Glover and Miss Cordelia Archer, "co-eds" at Wilberforce college, Green county, are home for the holidays."

Figure 11: 22 Dec 1904, Akron Beacon Journal.

"William R. Green and Miss Ethel Glover were united in marriage at the home of the bride's mother in the Seiberling building Thursday evening, February 9. The ceremony was conducted in the presence of but a few friends and relatives and the marriage service was read by the groom's father, Rev. Green of Canton. The bride was, until recently, a state "co-ed" at Wilberforce and the groom is an employe of the Hotel Buchtel."

Figure 12: Announcement of the marriage of William and Ethel on 9th Feb, 1905. 11 Feb 1905, Akron Beacon Journal.

THEY MOVED MANY TIMES (1903-1930)

"One of the most delightful New Year events was the pretty party given by Mr. and Mrs. Harry E. Hailstock in their new home, 225 Silver street, Thursday afternoon from 2 to 5 o'clock, in honor of their niece, Miss Virginia Hailstock of Swickley, Pa. The afternoon was spent in playing various Christmas games, after which an elaborate lunch was served by the hostess. Those present were: Misses Susan Lyons, Bertha Anderson, Sadie Glover, Stella Anderson, Elinor Hawley, Louise Broady, Julia McConico, Ruth Smith, Harriet Alexander, Helen Smith, Pandora McConico, Beatrice Lyone, Ursla Campbell, Virginia Hailstock and Messrs. Leonard Mitchel, James McConico, Anderson Archer, and Geradl Michell of Pittsburg."

Figure 13: New Year's Celebration 2 Jan 14 Akron Beacon Journal

THEY MOVED MANY TIMES (1903-1930)

News of Interest to Colored Citizens by Hannibal B. Lyons

"Mrs. Cora Jackson has accepted the position of assistant matron at Phyllis Wheatley Home for colored working girls at Cleveland. She began her duties last Monday.

The fifth anniversary of the opening of Wesley Mause will be held at the A.M.E. Zion church, Monday evening, Feb. 3rd. The following program is to be rendered which should make the evening's entertainment most interesting: Solos, Mrs. Allen Brown, **Mrs. Raymond Glover**, Mr. C.C. Pollard; Duets, Mr. and Mrs. L. T. Pinn, Miss Addie Moore and Mrs. William Ferguson. The speakers of the evening are Hon. B. F. Steward, Norwalk, O., **Mrs. Ethel Green**, Mrs. George Welsey, Frank B. Lancaster, H. B. Lyons and Rev. E. D. Bell. An elaborate supper will be served by the ladies of the church."

Figure 14: News of Interest to Colored Citizens, 2 Feb 1914, Akron Beacon Journal

Some interesting notations in this article Mrs. Jackson, a friend of the Glovers, becomes an assistant matron. Ethel in years to come will work there. Mrs. Raymond Glover (Aunt Mattie) could sing. And Ethel pays a visit to Akron and gives a speech.

> **Earl Stevens, Colored, is Assessed $200 Fine. Goes to Works.**
>
> Earl Stevens, an 18-year-old solored boy, who was indicted by the grand jury on the charge of assault and battery, had his hearing before Judge R. M. Wanamaker this morning. He entered a plea of guilty and was fined $200 and costs and given a six months' sentence in the Canton workhouse. Both the fine and the workhouse sentence were suspended on good behavior upon the recommendation of Prosecutor Frank Rockwell.
>
> Stevens, who has but one leg, attended a dance given at the Gorge on May 30 by local colored people. It is said that he accused Addison Glover, another colored boy, of carrying beer to immoral women, and this started a fight in which Stevens used a knife with telling effect.

The escapades of Addison Glover 3 Oct 1911 - Akron Beacon Journal

Addison

By 1910, Addison, affectionately called Manny, was 16 (b.1894) and is listed in the City Directory as the head of household working as a laborer. It is believed he was the family's favorite child. By 1914, with the return of his older brother Raymond from Youngstown, he was working at Wagoner & Marsh. Addison is the one child where there were multiple pictures (see Appendix) of him as a young man and a few rather unwanted newspaper articles, starting as

THEY MOVED MANY TIMES (1903-1930)

early as 1911. Apparently, Addison got into a fight with Earl Stevens while trying to defend his name ("Boy Fined $200 for Assault"). Addison was cut close to the heart, but the wounds were superficial ("Boys Figure in Cutting"). Both were sent to the workhouse to pay off fines but were later released on good behavior. Even in 1916, at the age of 22, he and his friend Charles Redmond were caught driving someone else's car. They were sentenced to time in the workhouse, but received suspended
sentences with a $25 payment to the church and repairs to the car ("Were Freed When They Pay Church").

In 1917, Addison is inducted into the Army because of the United States joining WWI. He would be attached to the Machine Gunnery Battalion but discharged in March, 1918 on a 25% medical discharge. He would return to Akron and work as a bellhop at the Akron Hotel. The last event while he was alive that would make the papers was a he reports he made of having money stolen from him while staying at a club. Addison became extremely ill and passed away on 2 Aug 1919 from pneumonia and an enlarged heart. Though it is not stated on his death certificate, the Spanish Flu could have been the cause as it was afflicting the area and young people were especially affected. The bereavement that followed, was huge enough to post a thank you note ("Thank You Notice: Addison E. Glover") from the family to

THEY MOVED MANY TIMES (1903-1930)

those who participated in the care and funeral service which followed.

THEY MOVED MANY TIMES (1903-1930)

BOYS FIGURE IN A CUTTING

Blade Wielded by Earl Stevens Almost Fatal to Addison Glover.

Colored Youth Bound Over to Grand Jury Under $1,000 Bond.

Two mere boys figured in police court in a cutting case Wednesday morning. The fight occurred at the Gorge, late Tuesday evening, and the participants were colored boys Earl Stevens, 17, 108 Bartges street, is alleged to have stabbed Addison Glover, 158 Hill street, just over the heart and in the arm. Police say that had the knife struck Glover a trifle lower, it would have pierced his heart.

STEVENS BOUND OVER.

After hearing the evidence in the case Mayor Sawyer bound Stevens over to the grand jury under $1,000 bond. Stevens, who is a cripple, claims that he was defending himself, while Glover says that Stevens struck the first blow. Stevens' leg is cut off below the knee and he uses a stump leg. Glover was not seriously cut, and was able to appear in police court Wednesday morning. Glover claims Stevens told lies about him, and he says this started the fight.

Addison is injured in a fight 31 May 1911 - Akron Beacon Journal

THEY MOVED MANY TIMES (1903-1930)

"One of the conditions on which Charles Redmond and Addison Glover had their sentences to the workhouse suspended for operating a machine without the consent of the owner, was that each pay $25 to the colored church. They are also to pay for the repairs to the machine. The car belonged to Ed. Romilly, of the University club."\

Figure 15: Are Freed When They Pay Church, 14 Jul 1916, Akron Beacon Journal.

"Police looking for Samuel Kish, age 14, 1123 Rhodes ave., who Tuesday left his home taking with him $100 in money and $100 Liberty bond. His disappearance was reported by his mother.

While sleeping in the Colored club at 22 1/2 N. Howard st. last night, Addison Glover, 210 James st., had his pockets picked. Money amounting to $30 was taken. Police have one suspect who may be arrest some time Wednesday."

Figure 16: Boy Missing: Money Taken, 21 May 1919, Akron Beacon Journal Last article on Addi*son Glover before his passing.*

THEY MOVED MANY TIMES (1903-1930)

"We wish to extend our heartfelt thanks to the pastor, choir and friends who so kindly assisted in our bereavement, the sickness and death of our beloved brother and son, Addison L. Glover. Signed

Mrs. Sadie Glover,
Mrs. Ethel Greene,
Mr. Raymond Glover,
Miss Sadie Glover"

Figure 17: Thank you notice published in paper, 2 Aug 1919, Akron Beacon Journal

1919 would find the Glover family at 210 James Street. Sadie Mae, the last child living at home, started working as a clerk at D. Lewis. In February of 1920, Sadie graduated from high school ("Seventy-Five Students to Graduate from Central and South: List Is Given") and joined a new group for colored high school graduates. She also found a new position as a clerk at the O'Neil Company.

1922 was an eventful year. Raymond was working as an auto repairman and living at 972 Haynes Street. Sadie Mae would marry Willie Davis, Aura Davis' son, on 5 Mar 1922 (*Summit County, Ohio, Marriage Records, 1840-1980*). If the story is to be believed, they were promised to each other at a young age. Regardless, Willie Davis was the love of Sadie Mae. Sarah Louise Holmes Glover would pass away on the 7

THEY MOVED MANY TIMES (1903-1930)

Jul 1922 ("Obituary for Sarah Glover (Aged 59)") from stomach cancer. She was the first to have a headstone; on it after her name it simply said, "Mother".

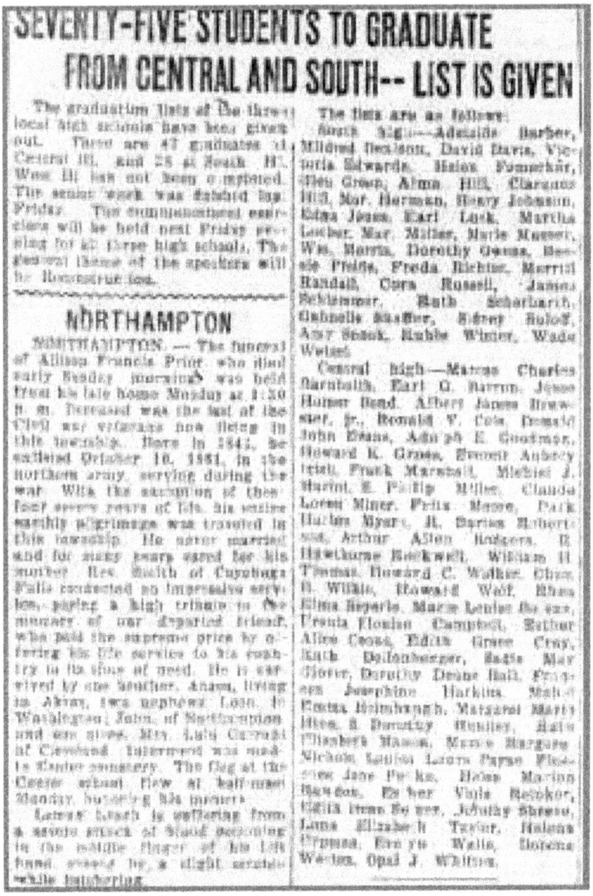

SEVENTY-FIVE STUDENTS TO GRADUATE FROM CENTRAL AND SOUTH-- LIST IS GIVEN

NORTHAMPTON

The lists are as follows:

Figure 18: Central High School graduation list, 4 Feb 1919, Akron Evening Times.

"One of the best projects yet developed among negroes of Akron is the formation of an organization composed of all colored people having had high school experience. The organization was perfected Wednesday evening at the Second Baptist church, with Miss Sadie Glover, president; Mr. Chester Tisdale, vice president, and Miss Ethel Black, secretary.

George W. Thompson, colored, Y.M.C.A, secretary is at present perfecting a program to be carried out by the high school body. He purposes to have the organization provide scholarships for students attaining marked intellectual achievement, to place the youth of the race in a better intellectual environment said to encourage young negroes to stay in school.

Figure 19: 20 Feb 1920, Akron Beacon Journal."

Sadie and William left for New York City. William sought work as a jazz musician. Sometime in 1925, Ethel visited them because Sadie was extremely ill. The Davises move to New York twice but return to Akron to stay sometime before 1930. Sadie would become involved with the Colored Women's Independent Voters' League as reported in 1927 ("Colored Women's Independent Voters' League: To Interview Municipal Candidates"). William worked as a continued to work as a musician but died from a pelvic abscess on 4 Jun 1930 at Peoples Hospital.

> "A committee to interview candidates in the municipal election was appointed at a meeting of the Colored Women's Independent Voters' league Tuesday night at the home of Mrs. Mary Woodson, 293 S. Broadway.
> Officers named at the meeting are: Mrs. C. H.

Parish, chairman; Mrs. Virginia Smith, secretary, and Mrs. Sadie Davis, vice-chairman.

The Next meeting will be held next Tuesday evening at the home of Mrs. J. R. Evans, 251 S. Broadway."

Figure 20:20 Jun 1927, Akron Beacon Journal

4

33 Chase Court (1930-1950)

During the next 15 to 20 years, the grandchildren of Louisa would be at their busiest (at least as is publicly known). Ethel returned to Akron sometime around 1928 and married Frank Washington. They would separate after two years, though their divorce wasn't final until 1941 ("Divorces Granted"). By then, Ethel and her second husband, Henry C. Wright, had lived in Detroit, Michigan for some years, at least since 1920. Ethel's oldest surviving son, Oliver William Greene (who went by the name Bill) would make Detroit his home, though there were accounts of his visits home. Henry C. Wright would die from a stroke in August 1926 leaving Ethel with an adopted infant son named Norman Henry Wright, the author's father. Ethel returned to Akron shortly after Henry's death. He would grow up in Akron and not leave until the war (WWII) except the many visits to Detroit. Ethel and Sadie became members of Wesley Temple AME Church and involved themselves in the many organizations that the church had, namely, Mary

33 CHASE COURT (1930-1950)

Exalted Temple, the Elks, the Neighborhood Clubs, 25 Year Club, and Optimistic 50. In 1933, their great-aunt Louisa Johnson Cleveland of Cincinnati, Ohio passed away. She left most everything to Ethel, her favorite niece (most likely the one she knew best since there was an eleven-year gap between sisters). This allowed Ethel to purchase a house on Chase Court. Sadie Mae Davis lived with her until she again married. The Chase Court neighborhood would be where Norman spent his childhood and where many of the friends, he made during this time lived. Raymond and Mattie Glover would also be involved though more quietly or less publicized. The Glovers had no children but fostered two girls during this time. For this family, reporting of their activities would also change from the primary venue of the Akron Beacon Journal to the Cleveland Call and Post starting around 1936. This may be due to not having an editor at the ABJ or because they lost their space. Some articles would continue in the ABJ, but for the most part the Call and Post was this family's main newspaper. The Call and Post had a section called 'the Northeast' or 'Central Akron News,' with Mrs. Moore the editor, which would report on the comings and goings of the black families in Akron. Norman

33 CHASE COURT (1930-1950)

Through the Depression years, though times were difficult, Ethel and Sadie lived at Chase Court and worked. And thus, Most of the early newspaper

> **SOCIAL NOTES**
>
> On Thursday, Aug. 8 an elaborate dinner was given at the home of Mrs. Ethel Wright of Chase Ct, in honor of Mother Aura Davis, Mr. Oliver Green and little Norman Wright. It was the birthday celebration of Mother Davis and little Norman. Mr. Green is of Detroit and is the son of Mrs. Wright. He came to Akron Sunday to visit his mother. Sixteen guests were present at the dinner consisting of fried chicken, meat loaf, macaroni salad, mashed potatoes, fried corn, sliced cucumbers, combination salad, ice cream, coffee cake and cookies. The dinner was a huge success.

Figure 21: Most likely sent in by Ethel who always called her son William by his given name, Oliver. Cleveland Call and Post 15 Aug 1935. Image published with permission of ProQuest LLC. Further reproduction is

accounts about Norman were social such as Norman's birthday party in 1935 at ten (Hicks). He celebrated it with "Mother" Aura Davis.

Other events such as the summer travel of Norman who spent time with his older brother in Detroit ("Central Akron News"), not just this one year, but many (Moore) would be reported. Norman would be mentioned as he participated in concerts given by the

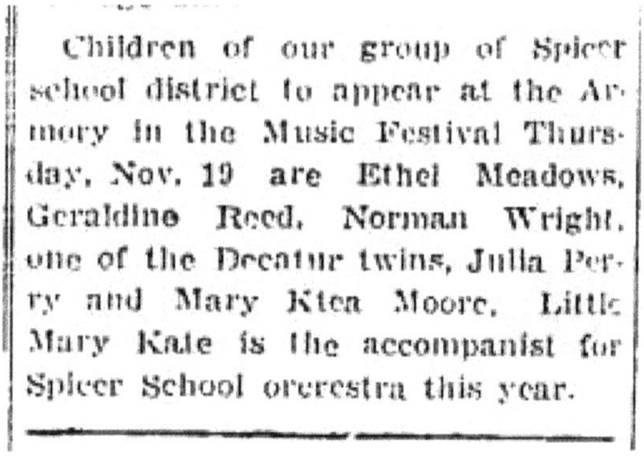

33 CHASE COURT (1930-1950)

> Children of our group of Spicer school district to appear at the Armory in the Music Festival Thursday, Nov. 19 are Ethel Meadows, Geraldine Reed, Norman Wright, one of the Decatur twins, Julia Perry and Mary Kten Moore. Little Mary Kate is the accompanist for Spicer School orcrestra this year.

Figure 22: Northeast Akron News, 17 Sept 1936. Image published with permission of ProQuest LLC. Further reproduction is prohibited without

Mary Exalted Temple ("Daughter Ruler") or Spicer School.

He was noted for his soprano voice [by his own account] and he also played trumpet in the church, school and Elks band. Of particular note was the YMCA camp account in 1937 ("Akron Boys Return Home From Cedar YMCA Camp"). His Aunt Sadie helped transport the young men. Akron pools were segregated, but he learned how to swim. He was much smaller than his friends and peers and being an adept swimmer equalized the playing field. He would eventually obtain his Life Saver badge which he was enormously proud of in an age where being a Life Saver Swimmer was rare for people of color.

33 CHASE COURT (1930-1950)

AKRON BOYS RETURN HOME FROM CEDAR YMCA CAMP

The Akron contingent of the Cedar YMCA summer camp returned home, Monday, August 9th. Eighteen boys and five counsellors from the Association for Colored Community Work spent the week beginning August 3d in the Centerville Mills, Cleveland YMCA camp for all branches of the Cleveland "Y". The boys reported this to be the finest program every presented at camp. A great many of them spent most of their time in the well-guarded new swimming pool. Stanley Kelly pleased his parents greatly by bringing home three belts and three pocketbooks and other articles that he had made in the handicraft shop. Bobbie Meaux surprised his mother by entering the 50 yard swimming race and proving to her that he could swim by making a good showing in the race. All the Akron boys entered into the activities whole heartedly and many stated that they are going to start immediately to prepare for next camp program.

Rubber City Lodge No. 233 of the IBPOE of W. sent two boys to this camp. The Community Center expresses gratitude to Mrs. J. B. Denis, Mrs. Sadie Davis, Mr. Henry Sparks, Mr. Rufus L. Thompson, Mr. Fred Scrutchings, Mr. Henry Haines, and Mrs. Mary B. Kelly for furnishing their cars to transport the boys to and from camp.

Those boys who attended camp this season through the ACCW included James, Clarence and Robert Blair, Stanley and Samuel Kelly, Robert and William Lykes, Harry and Allen Jackson, Sanford Meaux, Vaughn Parrish, Charles Miller, Norman Wright, Ernest Haines, Garland Parker and Chas. Wilson from Columbus, Ohio; Dickie Sparks; and Junior Smart (overnight.)

Counsellors who attended camp were Henry C. Sparks, Rufus L. Thompson, Samuel Thomas, Eddie Reilly, and Raymond R. Brown.

Mrs. Raymond R. Brown and her two daughters, Dolores and Barbara, spent the week-end with other counsellor's wives at the camp.

Norman was 12 when he went to this YMCA camp. Harry and Allen Jackson neighbors and friends along with Vaughn Parrish. 12 Aug 1937 - Cleveland Post. Image published with permission of ProQuest LLC. Further reproduction prohibited without permission

Figure 23:

33 CHASE COURT (1930-1950)

The Akron Beacon Journal has two pictures of Norman during one year of the Soap Box Derby in 1940. Both of which were perceived to be less than kind, but more in the way white papers viewed people of color ("Soap Box Derby Picture"). His mother kept the one that made the front page in 1941 and was less offensive ("Derby Racers Are 'King For A Day'"). Norman would graduate in Jan 1944 and join the Army Air Corps. He wouldn't show up in the local papers until released from duty in 1946 ("Civilians Again: 101 More Hunt for Suits"). Norman would be recalled to active duty in 1951. He would choose to make the Air Force his career choice. It was the practice of the military to post promotions in the hometown paper. His mother would move to Cleveland by 1951, so the Cleveland paper clipping is the one she kept.

33 CHASE COURT (1930-1950)

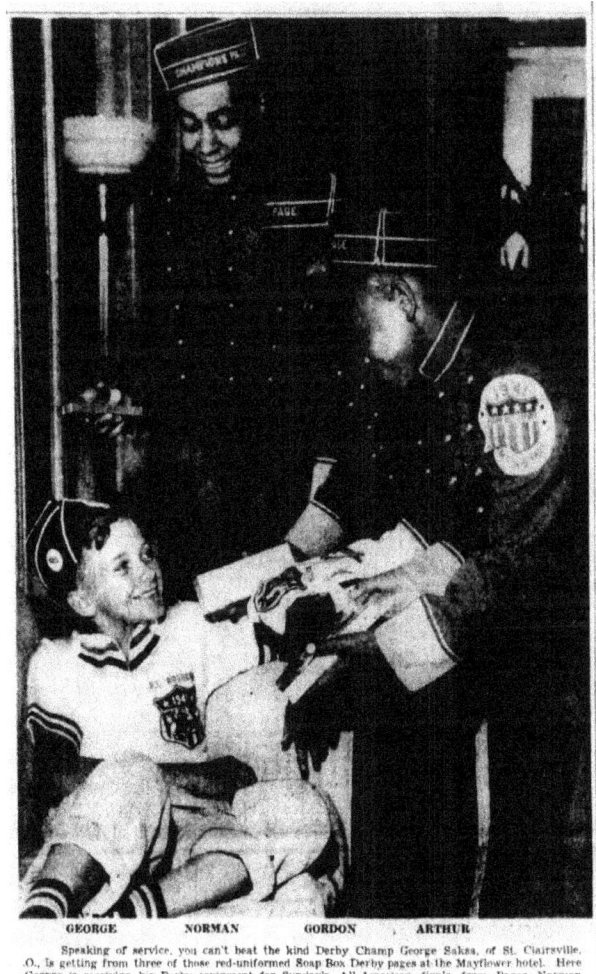

Figure 24: 16 Aug 1941, Akron Beacon Journal, pg. 1.

Mary Exalted Temple No. 95, The Optimistic 50, 1943 and the 25 Year Club

Figure 25: Optimistic 50 Club taken at the Elks Club. Ethel is 4th from left, front row. Undated, Ethel's Scrapbook.

33 CHASE COURT (1930-1950)

The Daughters of the Mary Exalted Temple no.95 were attached to the Improved Benevolent and Protective Order of Elks of the World (otherwise known as the Black Elks) Rubber City Lodge no. 233. Ethel was very active having been a Past Daughter Ruler ("Mary Exalted Temple"). The Elks started in Cincinnati in 1894 and by 1936, the Akron Temple membership was over 100 ("Daughter Ruler"). As an outgrowth of this, "The Optimistic 50" was born. Mrs. Harriet Bowie then Daughter Ruler organized the Optimistic 50 in 1939. One of the requirements for membership was being a financial member of the Temple. They would hold dances yearly at the Elks Ballroom usually in February ("AKRON NEWS"). Ethel would hold in her scrapbook pictures taken probably from one of those dances.

Sadie busied herself working as a teacher for the Works Project Administration (WPA) (Kingsberry), but she also spent her time being President of Neighborhood no. 4 [Chase Court] (Thompson), helping students learn Negro History during the summer (Stewart), attending a Business and Industry Girls Conference in 1937 at the Phillis Wheatly in Cleveland ("Akron Delegation to B&I Girls Conference"), and helping the NAACP in a membership drive ("NAACP Honors Graduates").

33 CHASE COURT (1930-1950)

The Chase Court Neighborhood Club 21 Dec 1946- Cleveland Call and Post Image published with permission of ProQuest LLC. Further reproduction is prohibited without permission.

Figure 26: 26 Sep 1938, Akron Beacon Journal, courtesy of Ethel Wright.

One of the organizations to which both sisters belonged was the Twenty-five Year Club. The club was founded in 1935 and was open to persons who had been in Akron 25 years or more. Honorary members had to be 70 years old and a resident of Akron for 25 years or more (Pitts). For the first anniversary celebration in April, Sadie emceed the program held at Second Baptist Church due to Ethel's illness.

33 CHASE COURT (1930-1950)

The highlight of this organization had to be the building of the fountain, stone base and walkway to the John Brown Memorial in Akron. The original monolith had been in place since 1914 in Perkins Park where John Brown kept his sheep. The 25 Year Club raised funds and had grand celebrations covered by the Akron Beacon Journal several times, on 24 Feb 1938 ("Wilberforce Singers Help John Brown Memorial Plan"), and on 26 Sep 1938 ("Memorial to John Brown Is Dedicated"), and ("Negroes Present Fountain to City: Great Niece of Abolitionist Takes Part In Perkins Woods Unveiling"). The program (McClain) was saved and is found on the last page of McClain's thesis. It shows Ethel as a VP and Sadie as Financial Secretary. It also shows the many dignitaries, including John Brown's niece, who attended the unveiling. No documentation has been found on how they raised the funds other than through the Wilberforce Singers, but it left a lasting legacy.

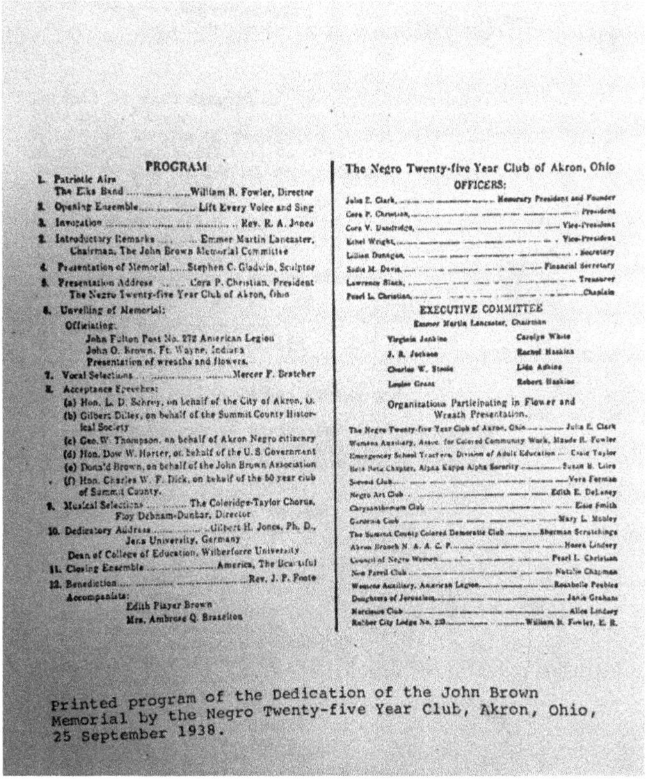

33 CHASE COURT (1930-1950)

Figure 27: 25 Sep 1938. Last page of Shirla
McClains' doctoral manuscript

This program probably represents the "Who's Who" of the Negro population in Akron and was included in the manuscript of Shirla McClain's doctoral thesis. Ethel, and her sister are listed as officers.

There were other groups and organizations that Ethel and Sadie belonged to, like the Organization of Colored Community Work where Sadie was an adult educator ("Akron Citizens Present Scroll of Honor to Local Undertaker") and the Federation of Women's

33 CHASE COURT (1930-1950)

Clubs, of which Ethel was a member ("Akron News"). By 1940, Sadie had remarried (Allie

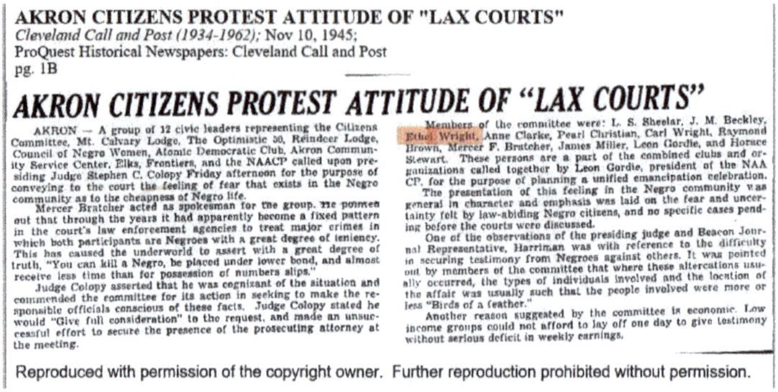

> **AKRON CITIZENS PROTEST ATTITUDE OF "LAX COURTS"**
> *Cleveland Call and Post (1934-1962);* Nov 10, 1945;
> ProQuest Historical Newspapers: Cleveland Call and Post
> pg. 1B
>
> ## AKRON CITIZENS PROTEST ATTITUDE OF "LAX COURTS"
>
> AKRON — A group of 12 civic leaders representing the Citizens Committee, Mt. Calvary Lodge, The Optimistic 50, Reindeer Lodge, Council of Negro Women, Atomic Democratic Club, Akron Community Service Center, Elks, Frontiers, and the NAACP called upon presiding Judge Stephen C. Colopy Friday afternoon for the purpose of conveying to the court the feeling of fear that exists in the Negro community as to the cheapness of Negro life.
> Mercer Bratcher acted as spokesman for the group. The spokesmen set out that through the years it had apparently become a fixed pattern in the court's law enforcement agencies to treat major crimes in which both participants are Negroes with a great degree of leniency. This has caused the underworld to assert with a great degree of truth, "You can kill a Negro, be placed under lower bond, and almost receive less time than for possession of numbers slips."
> Judge Colopy asserted that he was cognizant of the situation and commended the committee for its action in seeking to make the responsible officials conscious of these facts. Judge Colopy stated he would "Give full consideration" to the request, and made an unsuccessful effort to secure the presence of the prosecuting attorney at the meeting.
>
> Members of the committee were: L. S. Sheelar, J. M. Beckley, Ethel Wright, Anne Clarke, Pearl Christian, Carl Wright, Raymond Brown, Mercer F. Bratcher, James Miller, Leon Gardie, and Horace Stewart. These persons are a part of the combined clubs and organizations called together by Leon Gardie, president of the NAACP. for the purpose of planning a unified emancipation celebration.
> The presentation of this feeling in the Negro community was general in character and emphasis was laid on the fear and uncertainty felt by law-abiding Negro citizens, and no specific cases pending before the courts were discussed.
> One of the observations of the presiding judge and Beacon Journal Representative, Harriman was with reference to the difficulty in securing testimony from Negroes against others. It was pointed out by members of the committee that where these altercations usually occurred, the types of individuals involved and the location of the affair was usually such that the people involved were more or less "Birds of a feather."
> Another reason suggested by the committee is economic. Low income groups could not afford to lay off one day to give testimony without serious deficit in weekly earnings.
>
> Reproduced with permission of the copyright owner. Further reproduction prohibited without permission.

Scruggs) and had a son. She continued through the early forties to be involved in Akron. Ethel—either as a member of the Optimistic 50 or as a representative of the Council of Negro Women—participated in a protest about Lax Courts, "conveying to the court the feeling of fear that exists in the Negro community as to the cheapness of Negro life" ("Akron Citizens Protest Attitude of 'Lax Courts'"). Having been published in the Cleveland Call and Post, it is interesting to note one of the representatives for the court was from the Akron Beacon Journal who proposed the problem may be of "birds of a feather".

Image published with permission of ProQuest LLC. Further reproduction is prohibited without permission.

There were a smaller number of articles appearing after 1945. Sadie had moved to Cuyahoga Falls, while by 1949 Ethel had moved to Cleveland. There Ethel first works as a dietician, then director at both the Phillis Wheatley Home and the Home for the Colored Aged

Figure 28: 10 Nov 1945, Cleveland Call and Post, pg. 1B.

33 CHASE COURT (1930-1950)

in Cleveland. Ray and Mattie Glover spend their entire adult lives in Akron and continue to live quietly, (i.e., no newspaper accounts). Norman, as stated before, left for WWII. When he returned in 1946, ever so briefly, he moved to Columbus to enroll at The Ohio State University. He would be recalled into service in 1949 and would spend the next twenty years in the United States Air Force (USAF) rising to the rank of Major. Marcus, Sadie's son, would also spend time in the USAF, eventually moving permanently to San Francisco. Both would return to visit while their parents were alive but never to live.

For the Parrishes, Christians, Jacksons, Greenes and Davises, Hailstocks and Steeles who were part of the time period of Sarah and her daughters, life continued. The author has been able to trace their descendants until 1940, following some members until they passed.

We, the descendants of the Glovers, were no longer there. Ethel passed away in 1968, in Cleveland. Raymond, in 1964. Sadie Mae, the last of that generation passed away in 1978 at the age of 78. The cousins, such as they were, have spread or fled. But for a time, we prospered there and I feel I know this Akron and could still call it home.

5

Tying Up Loose Ends

Fannie Hughes, Cleveland and the NAAMHC

There is a picture of Fannie—as a toddler sitting on her mother's lap—and her family at the National Museum of African American History and Culture (NAAMHC) in Washington DC. They were originally identified as Felix Richards' slaves. The NAAMHC had purchased the picture at auction. Amy Bertsche, who had befriended me years ago, had known about this picture as it started her research into the members of Julia Hughes' family. She helped the NAAMHC to identify the people in the picture. Once Amy Bertsche and I figured out our research on Julia was on the same person, we were then able to start on Cousin Fannie Hughes. The museum has the picture in several places located within the building, most notably above the elevator entrance. Because Amy had most of the research on the Virginia clan, she was able to identify Fannie with her mother, aunts and cousins.

Figure 29: NMAAHC visit, Oct 2016 My sister and I visiting the exhibit featuring Fannie Hughes in the National Museum of African-American History & Culture e Akron clan was in the photo.

The Cincinnati Connection

Louisa Johns(t)on Cleveland is somewhat of an enigmatic member. She was Julia Louisa's oldest known daughter with her partner Moses Johnston. Louisa married Edward Cleveland who, according to city directories, was a teacher and fireman. Louisa owned several homes, being the proprietress of several rooming houses when she and Edward divorced. Edward and Louisa had five children of which only two survived to adulthood, Nellie and William. Nellie would marry a William Hill, but that is all that can be found at this time. William Johnston, Louisa's son, would become known as a Professor, but it is unclear if it

is because he is listed as a foot doctor. Cincinnati had a lively social culture particularly through the churches such as Union Baptist Church of which she was a member. Much of old Cincinnati has been destroyed, but a picture of her last home before it was destroyed for 'urban renewal' is below. She and the rest of her family are buried in the Wausau Cemetery in Cincinnati.

TYING UP THE LOOSE ENDS

Figure 29: 722 Kenyon Ave, Cincinnati Museum Center Digital Photo Collection, Public domain.

This is a picture of Louisa's former home from the Cincinnati Museum Center. Before this section of town of about 25,800 people was razed for a highway, they took pictures for historical effect. This was known as the Kenyon-Barr area of Cincinnati, a predominately black area. - Cincinnati Museum Center Digital Photo Collection (ca 1958).

The Detroiters and John E W Thompson

Uncle Bill (Oliver William Greene) and Auntie Bee (Edverta Motley) would spend their adult lives in Detroit, becoming leaders in the Prince Hall Masons and Order of the Eastern Star, respectively. They would raise Edverta's nephews and a godchild before having their own son in 1950. Newspaper articles abound about Bill as he was the State Representative in Michigan for the Masons. Edverta's grandfather was John Edward West Thompson, OD MD. He served under the Cleveland presidency as one of the youngest US Ministers ever. A written account is about him has been published by the author.

6

Afterword

Our August vacations

Since my dad (Norman Wright) was a career officer in the Air Force, Akron was a visit home especially to see his mother every couple of years when possible. My mother's parents had passed away or absent, so stops in Canton were rare. For a short time in the late fifties, we were stationed in Battle Creek, Michigan. We were then stationed in London where we stayed for 3 years. When we returned to the United States in August of 1963, we first visited Ohio. We then visited Michigan, then to Maine where we spent the next 5 and ½ years. Every year or so, we'd pack up in August and head home (my Dad kept Ohio license plates until his retirement in 1968). The last time we travelled as a family was 1967. Dad's mother passed away in September of 1968 and we moved to Connecticut in February of 1969. The trips ended mostly because my Dad didn't get that much vacation time anymore (a month). We also were all getting older and so was that wonderful 1963 Rambler we travelled in.

My memories of Uncle Bill Greene in Detroit, Ethel's oldest son, were of a scary (he had a big, bass voice and was 6ft tall) guy. We were absolutely scared to death to see him when we returned from London. He, in the end, was a big, fuzzy bear and we adored him. He and his wife, Aunt Vert and Nanna (Vert's mother) gave us (the children) the run of the place much to my mother's chagrin. In fact, during the whole trip we got "spoiled'. Aunt Sadie and Uncle Allie lived on a farm in Randolph, Ohio where we played in the barn with puppies and hay. Sometimes our cousin Marcus was home; we got clay Indian heads from him. Visiting Uncle Ray and Aunt Mattie, who still lived in Akron, was constraining for us since there was nowhere to play and we had to sit ever so politely on the couch. I just remember how dark it was inside. Grandma Ethel lived in Cleveland, so there was always a meal and sleepovers. When we first returned from England, my sister had a full British accent. My grandmother took my sister to every friend she knew and made my sister talk. That was probably the only time I wanted to keep an accent. The last we saw of 348 Chase Court; Dad's childhood home was in 1964 or 67. We were able to walk down the middle of the street since it was basically a dead end. We stayed with the Davis' (Alexander) overnight. Most of these trips were for the children to be seen and not heard. That being rather constraining, the best memories were of the times we were outside, catching worms to go fishing with Uncle Bill or playing outside.

Where did it all go?

Today, as I visit Akron, there isn't much left of the places we went. Chase Court was demolished; Bluff St and Scott Avenue barely exist. 190 North Broadway (across from what would become Quaker Oats and near Perkins School) is gone. These were the familiar places to Norman and the rest of his family as he grew up in Akron Many of the addresses I can put on a Google map, but there is only a dot of where it a place might have been. I am grateful to the Akron Summit library for having the historical maps so I can trace their movements. Wesley Temple (AMEZ Church), the church which Ethel and Norman still survives.

AFTERWORD

Figure 30: Cousin Fanny Hughes Churchill (1861-1950), ca 1940. Property of author.

AFTERWORD

Figure 31: William Glover, 1860-1890. Copy of original owned by Marc Scruggs.

AFTERWORD

Figure 32: Elna (Naomi) Churchwell Young (1894-1972). Copy of original owned by Marc Scruggs.

AFTERWORD

Figure 33: Oliver William (Bill) Raymond Green(e), 1906-1980. Owned by author.

AFTERWORD

Figure 34: Addison Emanuel Glover, 1895-1917. Owned by author.

AFTERWORD

Figure 35: Martha (Mattie) Clark Glover (1892-1984), ca.1960.

AFTERWORD

Raymond William Glover 1886-1965

AFTERWORD

Ethel Louise Glover Wright 1889-1967

AFTERWORD

Sadie May Glover 1900-1987

AFTERWORD

Sarah (Sadie) Louisa Holmes Glover 1863-1922

AFTERWORD

William Ransom "Royal" Green(e) 1880-1971

AFTERWORD

Norman Henry Wright 1925-2006

AFTERWORD

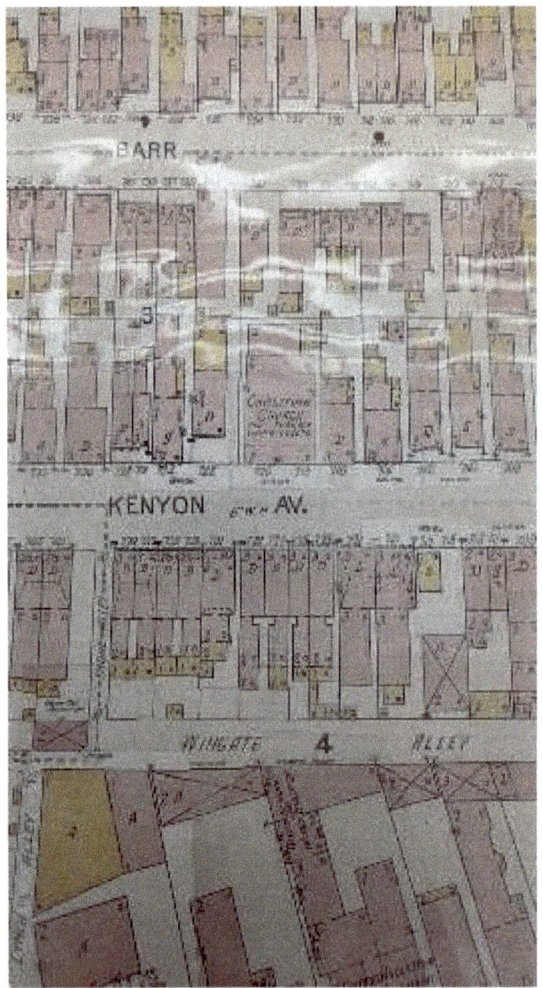

Kenyon-Barr area in Cincinnati, Ohio.

Bibliography

"License to Wed Before the Divorce Is Granted." Summit Beacon Journal, 13 Feb. 1889. newspapers.com, http://www.newspapers.com/image/228743284/?terms=christopher%2Bbailey.

"Akron Boys Return Home for Cedar YMCA Camp." *Cleveland Call and Post (1934-1962)*, 12 Aug. 1937, p. 12.

"Akron Citizens Present Scroll Of Honor to Local Undertaker." *Cleveland Call and Post (1934-1962).*, 29 June 1939, p. 9.

"Akron Citizens Protest Attitude of 'Lax Courts.'" *Cleveland Call and Post (1934-1962).*, 10 Nov. 1945, p. 1B.

"Akron Delegation to B&I Girls Conference. "*Cleveland Call and Post (1934-1962).*, 16 Dec. 1937, p. 12.

"Akron News: Federation Of Women's Clubs." *Cleveland Call and Post (1934-1962).*, 22 May 1943, p. 5_B.

"Akron News: Optimistic 50 Dance." *Cleveland Call and Post (1934-1962).*, 14 Feb. 1942, p. 7_B.

"Are Freed When They Pay Church." *The Akron Beacon Journal*, 14 July 1916, p. 14.

"Boy Fined $200 for Assault." *The Akron Beacon Journal*, 3 Oct. 1911, p. 3.

"Boys Figure in Cutting." *The Akron Beacon Journal*, 31 May 1911, p. 1. "Central Akron News." *Cleveland Call and Post (1934-1962).*, 8 Apr. 1937, p. 2.

City Directories for Toledo, OH. 1864.*fold3.com*, https://bit.ly/3qKC86R

"Civilians Again: 101 More Hunt for Suits." *The Akron Beacon Journal*, 30 Mar. 1946, p. 2.

"Colored Women's Independent Voters' League: To Interview Municipal Candidates." *The Akron Beacon Journal*, 20 July 1927, p. 21.

"Daughter Ruler." *Cleveland Call and Post (1934-1962)*, 19 Mar. 1936, p. 8.

"Death Notice: Addison Holmes." *The Summit County Beacon*, 7 Dec. 1881, p. 4.

"Derby Racers Are 'King For A Day'." *Akron Beacon Journal*, 16 Aug. 1941, p. 1.

Hicks, Jimmie. "Akron: Social Notes." *Cleveland Call and Post (1934-1962)*, 15 Aug. 1935, p. 7.

"Historic City Directories | Special Collections." *Akron-Summit County Public Library,* https://www.akronlibrary.org/locations/main-library/special- collections/genealogy/historic-city-directories. Accessed 18 May 2020.

Kingsberry, A. *Akron Negro Directory*. Kingsberry, 1940, https://www.akron-library.org/images/Divisions/SpecCol/images/Akron-Negro-Directory.pdf. Summit County Public Library, Special Collections.

"Mary Exalted Temple." *Cleveland Call and Post (1934-1962).*, 23 Sept. 1937, p. 11.

McClain, Shirla Robinson. *Contributions of Black in Akron: 1825-1975*. University of Akron, 29 May 1975.*Akron-Summit Public Library*, https://www.akronlibrary.org/images/Divisions/SpecCol/images/Con- tribution_-Blacks_Akron.pdf.

"Memorial to John Brown Is Dedicated." *The Akron Beacon Journal*, 26 Sept. 1938, p. 22. Newspapers.com.

Moore, Mrs. "Northeast Akron News." *Cleveland Call and Post (1934-1962)*, 17 Sept. 1936, p. 7.

"NAACP Honors Graduates." *Cleveland Call and Post (1934-1962).*, 17 June 1937, p. 12.

"Negroes Present Fountain to City: Great Niece of Abolitionist Takes Part In Perkins Woods Unveiling." *The Akron Beacon Journal*, 26 Sept. 1938, p. 22.

"Obituary for Sarah Glover (Aged 59)." *The Akron Beacon Journal*, 7 July 1922, p. 25.

Pitts, Verna. "Twenty-Five Year Club Celebrates Its First Anniversary." *Cleveland Call and Post (1934-1962); Cleveland, Oh.*, 23 Apr. 1936, p. 10.

"Sarah Meets Sister." *The Summit County Beacon*, 14 Nov. 1888, p. 5.

"Seventy-Five Students to Graduate from Central and South: List Is Given." *Akron Evening Times*, 4 Feb. 1919, p. 13.

"Soap Box Derby Picture." *Akron Beacon Journal*, 9 Aug. 1940, p. 26.

Stewart. "Baptists Study Negro History." *Cleveland Call and Post (1934-1962).*, 2 Sept. 1937, p. 12.

Summit County, Ohio, Marriage Records, 1840-1980. Summit County, Ohio, 1922. *www.ancestry.com*, https://bit.ly/3IGiVcA

"Thank You Notice: Addison E. Glover." *The Akron Beacon Journal*, 9 Aug. 1919. *Newspapers.com*, https://bit.ly/3lmLQIm.

Thompson, Juella. "Akron Call-Post Society: Neighborhood Club Repeats Party." *Cleveland Call and Post (1934-1962).*, 16 Dec. 1937, p. 11.

"Wilberforce Singers Help John Brown Memorial Plan." *The Akron Beacon Journal*, 24 Feb. 1938, p. 14.

Wright, Norma. "Tracing a Family History Using Newspaper Accounts." *Ohio Genealogy News*, vol. 49, no. 4, Winter 2018, pp. 28–31.

List of Figures

Figure 1: W-2 form for wages earned by Ethel Wright in 1944. Provided by author.19
Figure 2: Bailey's Akron Directory 1871-72. ....
Figure 3: A.R. Talcott&Sons City Directory, 1874, pg. 76. ....
Figure 4: Uncertified copy of Death Record obtained from Probate Office, Akron Ohio. Vol. 1 page 180. ....
Figure 5: Death notice for Christopher Bailey, Louisa Hughes' last husband -Akron Daily Democrat 29 Apr 1899 ....
Figure 6: The LLL was founded in Springfield, Ohio and had a column in the ABJ. 21 Jan 1903, Akron Beacon Journal. ....
Figure 7: Start of the Progressive Club, 21 Oct 1907, Akron Beacon Journal ....
Figure 8: 24 Jan 1908 Akron Beacon Journal...
Figure 9: William and Ethel Green with their son, James Theo ca. 1905. ....
Figure 10: The last entry in the local News column of Akron's Negro Citizens 10 Feb 1914, Akron Beacon Journal ....
Figure 11: 22 Dec 1904, Akron Beacon Journal. ....
Figure 12: Announcement of the marriage of William and Ethel on 9th Feb, 1905. 11 Feb 1905, Akron Beacon Journal. ....
Figure 13: New Year's Celebration 2 Jan 14 Akron Beacon Journal ....
Figure 14: News of Interest to Colored Citizens, 2 Feb 1914, Akron Beacon Journal ....
Figure 15: Are Freed When They Pay Church, 14 Jul 1916, Akron Beacon Journal. ....
Figure 16: Boy Missing: Money Taken, 21 May 1919, Akron Beacon Journal Last article on Addis*on Glover before*

his passing. ....
Figure 17: Thank you notice published in paper, 2 Aug 1919, Akron Beacon Journal ....
Figure 18: Central High School graduation list, 4 Feb 1919, Akron Evening Times...
Figure 19: 20 Feb 1920, Akron Beacon Journal." ....
Figure 20:20 Jun 1927, Akron Beacon Journal ....
Figure 21: Most likely sent in by Ethel who always called her son William by his given name, Oliver. Cleveland Call and Post 15 Aug 1935. Image published with permission of ProQuest LLC. Further reproduction is prohibited without permission...
Figure 22: Northeast Akron News, 17 Sept 1936. Image published with permission of ProQuest LLC. Further reproduction is prohibited without permission. ....
Figure 23: Norman was 12 when he went to this YMCA camp. Harry and Allen Jackson were neighbors and friends along with Vaughn Parrish. 12 Aug 1937 - Cleveland Call and Post. Image published with permission of ProQuest LLC. Further reproduction is prohibited without permission ....
Figure 24:16 Aug 1941, Akron Beacon Journal, pg 1. ....
Figure 25: Optimistic 50 Club taken at the Elks Club. Ethel is 4th from left, front row. Undated, Ethel's Scrapbook. ....
Figure 26: 26 Sep 1938, Akron Beacon Journal, courtesy of Ethel Wright. ....
Figure 27: 25 Sep 1938. Last page of Shirla McClains's doctoral manuscript ....
Figure 28: 10 Nov 1945, Cleveland Call and Post, pg 1B. ....
Figure 29: NMAAHC visit, Oct 2016 ....
Figure 30: 722 Kenyon Ave, Cincinnati Museum Center Digital Photo Collection, Public domain. ....
Figure 31: Cousin Fanny Hughes Churchill (1861-1950), ca 1940. Property of author. ....
Figure 32: William Glover, 1860-1890. Copy of original owned by Marc Scruggs. ....
Figure 33: Elna (Naomi) Churchwell Young (1894-1972). Copy of original owned by Marc Scruggs..
Figure 34: Oliver William (Bill) Raymond Green(e), 1906-1980. Owned by author. ....
Figure 35: Addison Emanuel Glover, 1895-1917. Owned by author. ....
Figure 36: Martha (Mattie) Clark Glover (1892-1984),

ca.1960. Owned by author...

II

Addendum

This is a reprint of an article published by the Ohio Genealogical Society. Originally written for a 'contest' which was lost. But this is a good story and I was approached to have it published in their journal for which I am eternally grateful. This started my journey of searching for articles on this family and though part two of this book, it is the prequel to the Holmes family story in Akron, Ohio.

9

Tracing A Family History Using Newspaper Accounts

Introduction

While growing up, my family would have great conversations at the dinner table about our family history. Both my parents grew up in the Canton-Akron area with each being from one of those cities. My mother's family came from Alabama in the 1920s, my father's family came to Ohio in the mid-1800's. My father's story included an escaped slave named Louisa. It is that story, in part, I discovered using newspapers such as Akron Beacon Journal, the Akron Daily Democrat, the Plain Dealer and the Mansfield News. These newspapers are immeasurably important in discovering missing pieces of the story. A quick note, the citations included here are current; having lost or having the original citations invalidated

TRACING A FAMILY HISTORY USING
NEWSPAPER ACCOUNTS

by updated technologies.

An Intriguing Beginning

In the early 1980's, my father's cousin, Marc came to visit us. Marc imparted some family knowledge and a newspaper clipping (see below) he had acquired. This clipping was the impetus to seriously research this side of my family over the next thirty years.

> "Mrs. Julia Hughes, who is said to have been 109 years, died at her home 190 1/2 North Broadway Saturday evening of old age. Previous to Mrs. Hughes' death there are four generations living at her house as follows: Mrs. Hughes, her daughter, Mrs. Louisa Bailey, who is 60 years old; her granddaughter, Mrs. Sadie Glover and her four children, the eldest being 15 years old...Alexandria, Va., and she claimed to have seen George Washington. For many years she had been blind, yet always of a pleasant disposition and had the typical manner of southern 'mammy.' She was born in slavery and located in Akron in 1876 to live with her daughter, Mrs. Bailey.
>
> Funeral services are held Tuesday at 2 o'clock at the residence. Internment in Glendale cemetery."

TRACING A FAMILY HISTORY USING NEWSPAPER ACCOUNTS

- *(Akron Beacon Journal)*

Discoveries

I continued to collect information via Ancestry, FamilySearch and other online repositories. I made several trips to the Akron-Summit Public Library. I found a shorter version of the Beacon Journal article in the Mansfield News dated around the same time (i.e., 5 March 1902). Having done extensive work on another relative, I realized that newspapers are taking copies from another source and that if that primary source could be located, I might find the original article.

With the assistance of friend and fellow researcher, Amy Bertsche, re- searching the family of Julia Hughes in Alexandria, Virginia we found the original article in the Akron Daily Democrat [This is included in the Library of Congress' Chronicling America collection]. It is a lengthy, front-page article which confirmed family history facts and is partially quoted below:

> *"...She belonged to a family named McCrea, and like all Southern negroes who are well treated by their*

TRACING A FAMILY HISTORY USING NEWSPAPER ACCOUNTS

owners, she adored the family, still, when freedom came, she welcomed it as the happiest moment in her life, and it was a joyful day when her daughter could offer her a home at her own reside. In 1876, she came to Akron to live with her daughter, Mrs. Bailey." – (Akron Daily Democrat.)

The article though very descriptive of Julia, doesn't mention how she came to be with her daughter or account for Louisa being an escaped slave. Could there be other documented accounts?

The indexing of several newspapers, particularly the Akron Beacon Journal made my search easier, and copies could be sent via email. Through this experience I learned that the world of my ancestors could be discovered. A breakthrough came with "A Story of Separation":

"...Mrs. Louisa Holmes (colored) of Akron, Ohio, who was sold away from her mother forty years ago, while in slavery, grew up away from her parent and finally escaped and came north finally settling in Akron, Ohio. On Thursday, Mrs. Holmes started for Alexandria, Va., where she finally learned that her now aged

mother was staying, with the intention of bringing the latter north to pass the remainder of her days."
— *("Clipped From Holmes County Republican").*

This article tells me that she was able to find her mother (though not how) and that she brought her to Ohio. The original piece in the Beacon, however, confirmed the family story of Louisa being an escaped slave. (Louisa married several times, one being after the death of her husband, Addison Holmes in 1881, hence the different surname.)

One more article from the *Summit County Beacon* confirmed that Julia arrived safely back with her mother in Akron.

"-Some weeks since, The BEACON contained the account of the departure of a colored lady of this city — Mrs. Louisa Holmes — in search of her aged mother from whom she had been separated in slavery when a child, and whom she had not seen for forty years. We are pleased to state that Mrs. H succeeded in finding her mother in Alexandria, Va, and that she the happily reunited couple arrived home safely this morning."
("Clipped from The Summit County Beacon").

TRACING A FAMILY HISTORY USING
NEWSPAPER ACCOUNTS

Analyzing These Discoveries

It is difficult to determine whether the early members of the family are sufficiently well known enough to rate a mention in the social news, or whether the short stories appeared because of the pathos of the family reunification story. They certainly are not in the social "blue book" of the day. None of the previous articles are compiled into a larger, more comprehensive story by the Akron Beacon Journal. Not until 1902 would the Akron Democrat compile something beyond a short obituary. Even that paper missed this article that appeared in the Akron City Times in 1885, relating that Julia had reunited with another daughter from New Orleans.

> *"Mrs. Julia Elyard, of New Orleans, came to Akron some two weeks ago on the hunt for her mother and sister, whom she was parted from in 1845... Mrs. Elyard came on to Akron and here found her mother and sister, her sister being Mrs. Louisa Holmes. The daughter recognized the mother on sight. They talked of their old home in Virginia, and of the incidents there enacted."*
> – *("Clipped From Akron City Times").*

It is unclear even to this day, why this particular family

TRACING A FAMILY HISTORY USING NEWSPAPER ACCOUNTS

was so notated in their city. There is no evidence of a higher social status among Akronites. Research has found the family arrived in Akron shortly after the Civil War. They are among the early 'colored' settlers. Given that there are no headstones for any of the family until 1922, I would dare say, they are not well off.

There are at least five other newspaper articles that document the lives of this family including two accounts of Julia's grandson, Addison Glover. Two decades after the death of Julia Hughes, her great grand-daughter, Ethel Glover Wright, would use the newspaper to account of the social actions of her family members and social groups to which she belonged. This is a great historical path and one that should not be ignored even in the marginal paths of society.

Bibliography

Akron Beacon Journal (Ohio) 4 Mar 1902, p.3.

"Died at the Age of 109 Years," Akron Daily Democrat. Chroniclingamerica.loc.gov, http://chroniclingamerica.loc.gov/lccn/sn830281407. Accessed 8 Sept 2017.

News-Journal (Mansfield, Ohio), 5 Mar 1902, p.6 digital images *Newspapers.com* (www.newspapers.com:accessed 23 Nov 2017).

Akron City Times (Ohio), 26 Aug.1885, p.2 digital images *Newspapers.com* (www.newspapers.com:accessed 23 Nov 2017).

"A Story of Separation," *Holmes County Republican* (Millersburg, Ohio), 25 June 1874, p.3.

The Summit County Beacon (Akron, Ohio), 15 July 1874, p.3 digital images *Newspapers.com* (www.newspapers.com:accessed 23 Nov 2017).

www.ingramcontent.com/pod-product-compliance
Lightning Source LLC
Chambersburg PA
CBHW071724020426
42333CB00017B/2378